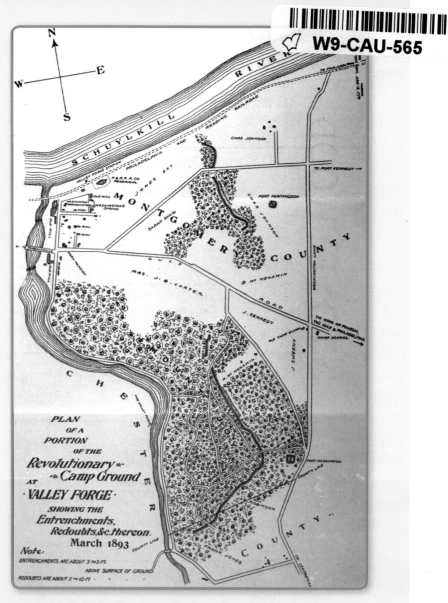

▲ Valley Forge was named for a forge in small village located where Valley Creek met the Schuylkill River.

October 4, 1777

Americans attack British Soldiers at Germantown, but are forced to retreat. The continental army camps at Whitemarsh until December 12.

December 19, 1777

The Continental Army reaches Valley Forge.

Harsh Weather

The weather at Valley Forge was worse than usual during the winter of 1777–1778. Snowfall was heavy. Within days of the Continental Army's arrival, the snow was six inches deep. Temperatures were often bitterly cold. When the cold let up, the snow turned into thick mud. Then the cold would return, freezing the rutted mud into icy ridges, leaving the campgrounds caked with dirty, muddy ice.

At first, the soldiers slept in tents. Then they built log huts. At least 12 soldiers lived in each hut. The officers were luckier. Their huts housed fewer people—usually between two to seven. Some officers roomed in nearby farmhouses. The huts turned out to be little better than the tents had been. They were tiny and cramped, and had soggy dirt floors and no windows. Fireplaces provided some heat. But they also filled the huts with thick smoke.

▼ **The Continental Army built about 1,000 huts at Valley Forge.**

▲ Actors re-enact what it was like to be at Valley Forge during the winter of 1777–1778.

Without proper shelter or clothing, troops suffered terribly in the cold weather. Many lost their feet to frostbite. One officer wrote that the Continental soldiers

"were in want of everything . . . they had neither coats, hats, shirts, nor shoes . . . their feet and legs froze till they became black, and it was often necessary to amputate them."

So many soldiers did not have shoes that one soldier said that the British would be able to "track the army by the blood from their feet."

A Shortage of Supplies

The Continental Army's supply problem quickly grew worse. Patriot supporters had hidden weapons for the soldiers at Valley Forge, but the British found them first. The British troops took everything they could and burned what little they left behind.

Bad roads added to the problems. Muddy roads and broken-down bridges often kept supplies from reaching the troops. An important officer in charge of delivering supplies to Valley Forge— and making sure the roads were in good shape—was accused of ignoring his job.

It took about 34,500 pounds of meat and 168 barrels of flour per day to feed the army. Many of the local farmers did not want to exchange food for the nearly worthless Continental money.

Soldiers often had only hard "fire cakes" to eat. These were made by cooking a paste of flour and water on a rock or in the fire's ashes. Sometimes, soldiers had nothing to eat but what they could find in nearby forests and fields.

Cold and hungry soldiers at Valley Forge ▶

VALLEY FORGE

6 7 8 9 10   805   11 10 09 08

Harcourt
SCHOOL PUBLISHERS

Visit *The Learning Site!* www.harcourtschool.com

Hard Times From the Start

▲ General George Washington

By the winter of 1777, the spirits of the Continental Army were low. The Patriots had lost several battles in the revolution, and they were tired. The soldiers needed a safe place to camp for the coldest months of the year. General George Washington chose Valley Forge, Pennsylvania, as the site for the Continental Army's winter camp.

Washington chose Valley Forge because of its high, flat location. From there soldiers could easily look for enemies. At 22 miles away from Philadelphia, Valley Forge was a safe distance from the city. At the same time, it was still close enough for the Americans to keep an eye on the British who were spending the winter there. Much of the camp was surrounded by water. Attackers would have to cross Valley Creek or the Schuylkill River before charging uphill to reach the camp.

When Washington's army of about 11,000 soldiers reached Valley Forge, they did not have many supplies. They were short of food, clothing, and weapons. Soon, cold weather, transportation problems, poor leadership, and terrible diseases made their lives harder.

The Journey to Valley Forge

September 11, 1777

At the Battle of Brandywine, American soldiers fail to stop the British from moving toward Philadelphia, the colonial capital.

September 24, 1777

The British take control of Philadelphia.

You call this a feast?

On orders from Congress, the Continental Army at Valley Forge celebrated a late Thanksgiving dinner on December 18, 1777. Instead of feasting on turkeys and pies, the soldiers had only a half a cup of rice and a tablespoon of vinegar each! General Washington may have eaten his Thanksgiving meal with this fork and knife.

Conditions Bring Disease

Because of the dirty living conditions, diseases spread quickly at Valley Forge. The camp did not have toilets and there was no clean water. People—and their horses—relieved themselves wherever they wanted, even into the same water supply they used for drinking and cooking. One disease that is spread this way is dysentery.

▲ After the war, Yellow Springs became a popular health spa.

Another disease that spread through the camp at Valley Forge was typhus. Typhus is passed from person to person through infected body lice. Both dysentery and typhus are common when people are crowded together without the facilities they need to keep clean.

The soldiers at Valley Forge got sick easily because they were already weakened from hunger and cold. Temporary hospitals were set up, but there were not enough workers, medicine, or supplies. The crowding in the hospitals helped spread patients' illnesses to others. As many as 3,000 soldiers died in the camp or its hospitals.

Women at Valley Forge

Some of the soldiers' wives lived with the troops at Valley Forge. Many of them worked as nurses. Even General Washington's wife, Martha, joined her husband at Valley Forge. One person remembered how hard she worked, caring for the soldiers: "I never in my life knew a woman so busy from early morning until late at night as was Lady Washington, providing comforts for the sic soldiers." Other women at Valley Forge cooked, did laundry, and worked as house keepers for the officers.

The first true military hospital in the United States was built at Yellow Springs, Pennsylvania, in 1777 to care for soldiers at Valley Forge. There, German surgeon Dr. Bodo Otto and his two sons cared

Change Comes to Valley Forge

Nathaniel Green

Life began to improve at Valley Forge in the early months of 1778. One of Washington's best generals, Nathaniel Green, saw to the rebuilding of the roads and bridges that had blocked the flow of supplies into Valley Forge. Wagons began to arrive with food and clothing for the troops. Thomas Jefferson wrote that Nathaniel Green was "second to no one in enterprise, in resource, in sound judgement . . . and every other military talent."

Soon, a German-born baker named Christopher Ludwig came to Valley Forge. Working without pay, Ludwig and his workers made a pound of fresh bread per day for each soldier.

▼ Friedrich Wilhelm von Steuben drilling the Continental Army at Valley Forge.

Then, in April, thousands of shad fish began their yearly trip up the Schuylkill River to lay their eggs. Soldiers had all the fish they could eat. One observer noted, "For almost a month the whole camp stank [of fish] and men's fingers were oily."

By March, Friedrich Wilhelm von Steuben had arrived at Valley Forge to train the Continental Army. Unlike many generals, Steuben worked directly with the soldiers himself. Steuben spoke almost no English. But he spoke French, and so did several of Washington's staff. They translated his orders from French to English.

Steuben showed the Americans how to shoot and how to march. He also taught them to charge the enemy with the bayonet, the steel blade attached to the end of a musket. Before, most Continental soldiers had only used their bayonets for cooking over a fire! Steuben was tough, but the soldiers respected him. They learned his lessons quickly and soon grew into a skilled fighting force.

This statue of Friedrich Wilhelm von Steuben overlooks the grounds at Valley Forge. ▶

A Transformed Army

American soldiers worked hard at Valley Forge. In time they became a stronger and more skillful army. While the Americans trained, British soldiers spent their winter living comfortably in Philadelphia.

The British soldiers went to parties and plays. Benjamin Franklin joked that the British had not taken control of Philadelphia. Instead, he said, "Philadelphia has taken control of the British." Franklin meant that the British troops got used to the entertainment the city had to offer. While the Americans got tougher and more focused on their jobs, the British did just the opposite.

▲ The Continental Army became well-organized at Valley Forge.

The Continental Army left Valley Forge on June 19, 1778, when the British left Philadelphia. By then, the American soldiers were well-fed and well-trained. They were ready to make their move against the British. The two armies fought on June 28 at Monmouth Courthouse in New Jersey. The British retreated from the fight. The once ragtag group of men had become a professional army. The six awful months at Valley Forge had created soldiers were who were ready and able to win their country's independence from Britain.

Valley Forge Today

Today, people come to Valley Forge National Historic
Park to learn about the events of the terrible winter
of 1777–1778. Many of the original buildings at Valley
Forge still stand. Visitors can tour the Isaac Potts House,
which served as General Washington's headquarters.
They can also visit the Dewees's House, which was used
by soldiers as a place to cook food and repair weapons
and equipment. At these sites visitors learn what life
was like at Valley Forge. Also through re-enactments,
storytelling, demonstrations, and hands-on projects,
people can understand how much the soldiers suffered
that winter.

In recognizing the sacrifices the Continental Army
made at Valley Forge, George Washington said: "Naked
and starving as they are we cannot enough admire
the incomparable patience and fidelity of the soldiery."
People today are reminded of the soldiers' sacrifices
when they see these words on the National Memorial
Arch at Valley Forge National Historic Park. Other
monuments at Valley Forge honor the leadership of
individuals, such as those to General Freidrich von
Steuben and General Anthony Wayne.

**National Memorial Arch
at Valley Forge ▶**

NAKED AND STARVING AS THEY ARE
WE CANNOT ENOUGH ADMIRE
THE INCOMPARABLE PATIENCE AND FIDELITY
OF THE SOLDIERY
WASHINGTON AT VALLEY FORGE FEBRUARY 16, 1778

Think and Respond

1. How did Valley Forge's location make it a good spot for the Continental Army's winter camp?

2. How did the weather affect living conditions at Valley Forge?

3. What caused disease to spread at Valley Forge?

4. How was the Continental Army different after spending the winter of 1777–1778 at Valley Forge?

5. What might have happened if the British soldiers in Philadelphia had trained as hard as the Continental Army during the winter of 1777–1778?

 # Activity

With three of your classmates role play the following people who were at Valley Forge: a soldier in the Continental Army, General George Washington, Frederich Wilhelm von Steuben, and a British soldier in Philadelphia. Act out a conversation between these people in which each tells about their experiences at Valley Forge.